WHAT'S IN THE HOLE?
CRITTERS OF THE SONORAN DESERT

WITH NAMES IN THE LANGUAGES OF O'ODHAM, SCIENCE, SPANISH, AND ENGLISH

BY LISA MARIA BURGESS
PHOTOS BY DON BURGESS

Is it a **monster**?

Maybe.

Gila monsters **do** sleep in holes.

ciadagĭ
Heloderma suspectum
monstruo de Gila
Gila monster

Leave it alone because
it is venomous.

Is it a **snake**?

Maybe.

Diamondback rattlesnakes **do** go into holes to eat rats.

The bobcat sees the rattlesnake.
Do you?

The cactus wren
sees the rattlesnake.
Do you?

ko'owĭ
Crotalus atrox
víbora de cascabel de diamantes
western diamondback rattlesnake

Leave it alone.
Yes, it's venomous too!

Camouflage!

This snake is
moving fast!

What's in the hole?
The **doves** don't know, but they're curious!

ho:hoi
Zenaida macroura
paloma huilota
mourning dove

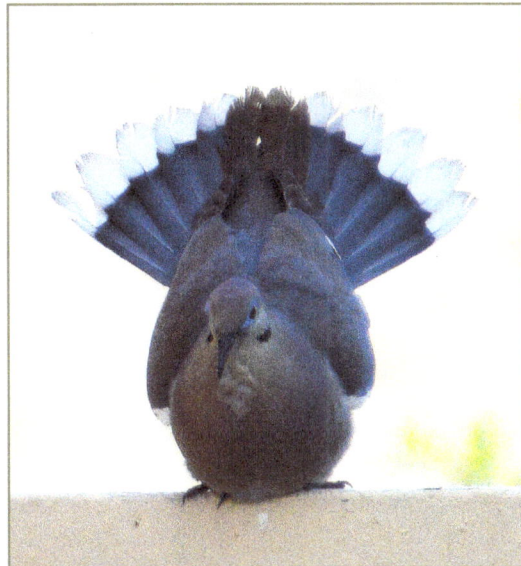

okokoi
Zenaida asiatica
paloma alas blancas
white-winged dove

Is it an **owl**?

Maybe.

Burrowing owls **do** nest in holes.

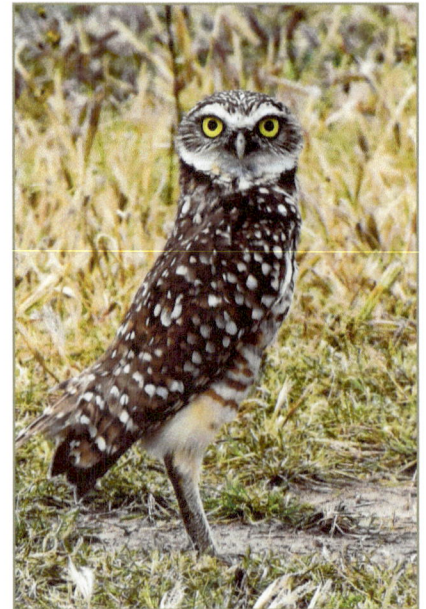

ku:kulul
Athene cunicularia
tecolote llanero
burrowing owl

This baby owl is running back to its nest in a hole!

Is it a **squirrel**?

Maybe.

Antelope squirrels **do** dig holes in which to stay cool.

cekol
Ammospermophilus harrisii
ardilla antílope de Sonora
antelope squirrel

Or a **lizard**?

Maybe.

Desert spiny lizards **do** borrow a burrow in which to cool off.

Or maybe a **toad**, digging out of the ground to enjoy the rain.

hiwinoḍ
Sceloporus magister
lagartija espinoso del desierto
desert spiny lizard

babad
Bufo alvarius
sapo del desierto de Sonora
Sonoran desert toad

Poisonous: don't touch.

Is it a **javelina**?

Definitely not!

Even baby javelinas are too big to squeeze into the hole.

tasi'ikol
Tayassu tajacu
pecarí
peccary or javelina

Is it a little **bee**?

Maybe.

Some bees **do** nest in holes.

pana:l
Anthophila
abeja
bee

A bee is smaller than a hummingbird, smaller than a moth: definitely small enough to live in the hole!

What's in the hole?

The **bobcats** don't know, but they're curious!

gewho
Lynx rufus
lince rojo
bobcat

Is it this **little lizard**?

Not likely.

The horned lizard tries to look scary, but it's delicate, so be careful.

cemamagĭ
Phrynosoma
lagartija cornuda
horned lizard

Is it a **tarantula**?
Maybe.
Tarantulas **do** nest in holes.
And no, not dangerous.

Camouflage!
This one is likely
a Santa Catalina
Mountain tarantula.
Can you see the legs
that look like sticks,
and the body that
looks like a pebble!

hiañ
Aphonopelma
tarántula
tarantula

What's in the hole?

The **quails** don't know, but they're curious! Even the babies are curious!

kakaicu
Callipepla gambelii
codorniz chiquiri
Gambel's quail

Is it a **ground squirrel**?

Maybe.

Round-tailed ground squirrels **do** dig holes, where they make nests and sleep.

şelig
Spermophilus tereticaudus
ardillón cola redonda
round-tailed ground squirrel

How many little ground squirrels can you count?

What's in the hole?

All the birds are curious!

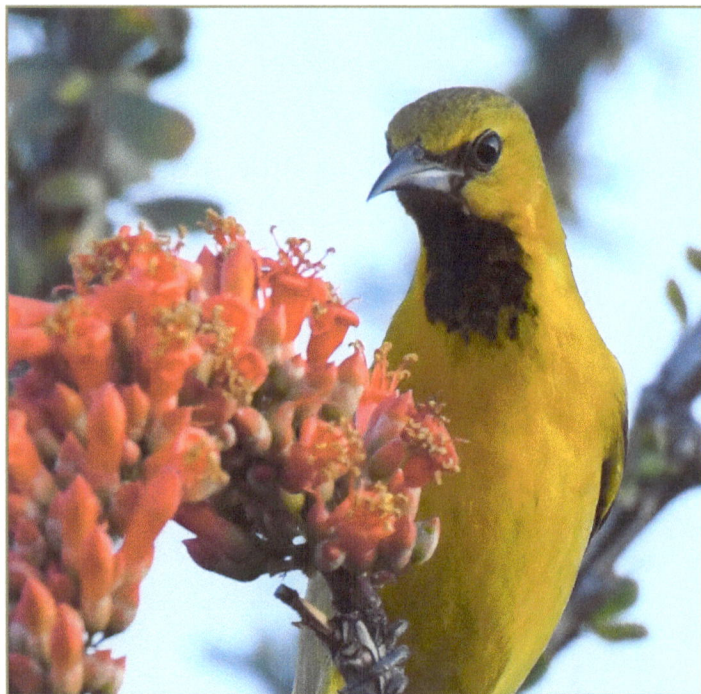

Can you find:
the cardinal,
the roadrunner,
the oriole, and
the curve-billed
thrasher?

How about
the peregrine falcon,
the great horned owls,
the pileated woodpecker
the Gila woodpecker,
and the ruby-throated
hummingbird?

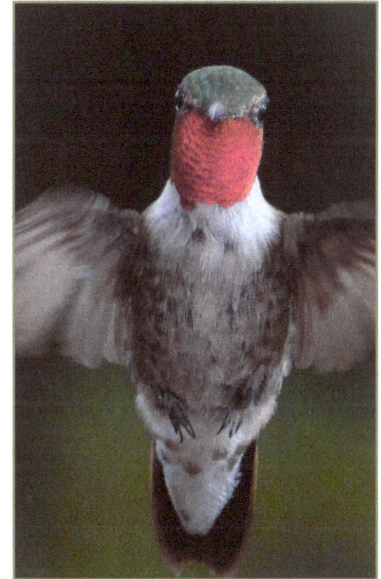

Even the hummingbird
hovered in order to
look!

What's in the hole?
All the animals are curious!

How many **mule deer** can you count?

Hint!

huawĭ
Odocoileus hemionus
venado mulo
mule deer

This **coyote** is passing through, but pauses for a closer look.

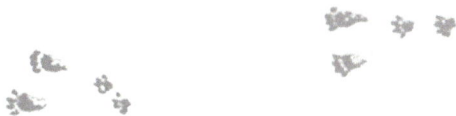

ban
Canis latrans
coyote
coyote

Is it a **rabbit**?

Yes!

Four baby cottontails were sleeping in the hole!

No, not a jackrabbit!

Yes, a cottontail!

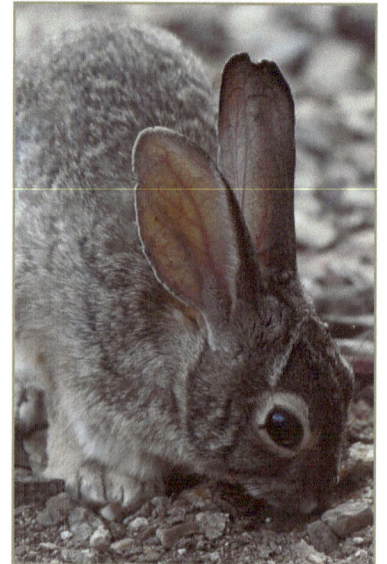

cuk cuːwĭ
Lepus californicus
liebre cola negra
black-tailed jackrabbit

toːbĭ
Sylvilagus audubonii
conejo del desierto
desert cottontail

Now the baby bunnies are sitting under the cacti, enjoying the morning.

Now the bunnies are back in their hole!

Rules of Observation

Should I put anything down the hole? No!
- No hands down the hole.
- No sticks down the hole.
- No poison down the hole.

Should I watch the hole? Yes!
- Be quiet.
- Sit away from the hole and watch.
- Photograph or draw the critter that comes out of the hole.

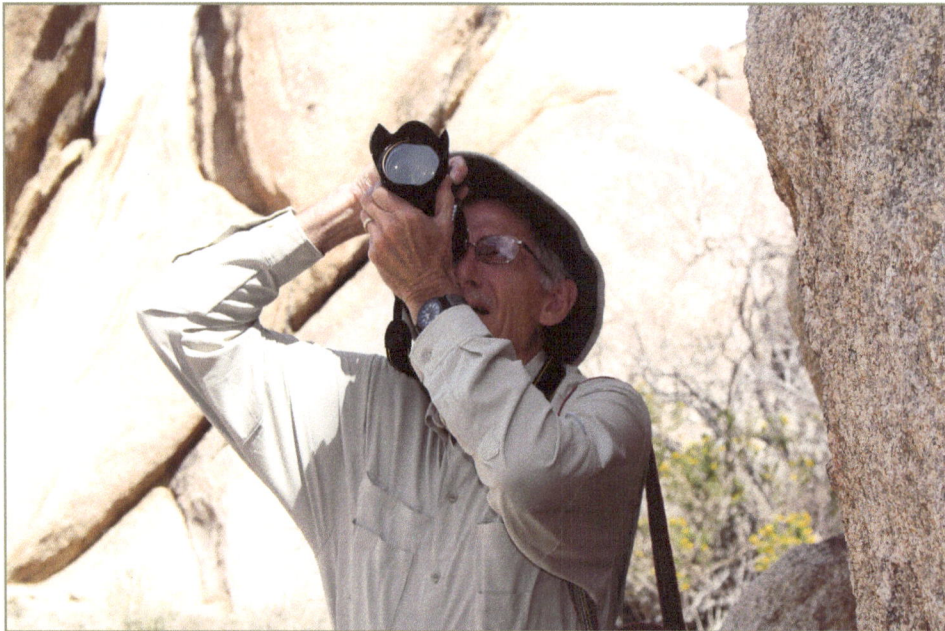

Don Burgess (1939-2022) photographed most of the wildlife portraits in this book behind his house north of Tucson, Arizona; he photographed the burrowing owls near Cuauhtémoc, Chihuahua. Also on the north side of Tucson, Bryan Wilson photographed the snake on the move and the tarantula, and Lisa Maria Burgess the bunnies in the hole. With thanks to Kristin Williams for photographing Don! And many thanks to Ronald Geronimo, Director of the O'odham Language Center, for providing names in O'odham, and to the staff at the Arizona-Sonora Desert Museum for their identification review.

Curious Birds

O'odham	Science	Spanish	English
wipismel	*Archilochus colubris*	colibrí garganta rubí	ruby throated hummingbird
sipuk	*Cardinalis cardinalis*	cardenal rojo	northern cardinal
taḍai	*Geococcyx californianus*	correcaminos norteño	roadrunner
cukuḍ	*Bubo virginianus*	búho cornudo	great horned owl
hikiwig	*Melanerpes uropygialis*	carpintero del desierto	Gila woodpecker
hikiwig	*Dryocopus pileatus*	carpintero pileado	pileated woodpecker
s-uam ṣaṣañ	*Icterus*	calandria	oriole
kulwicgam	*Toxostoma curvirostre*	cuicacoche pico curvo	curve-billed thrasher
wiṣag	*Falco peregrinus*	halcón peregrino	peregrine falcon
hokkaḍ	*Campylorhynchus brunneicapillus*	matraca del desierto	cactus wren

Photographs by Don Burgess, Bryan Wilson, Lisa Maria Burgess, and
Kristin Williams. Spanish edit by Héctor Cisneros Vázquez. Design by LM B. Noudéhou.
Published by Barranca Press.

ISBN PB: 978-1-939604-58-3
Library of Congress Control Number: 2023951825

Subject Areas: Juvenile Nonfiction
Animals / Burrowing Animals
Animals / Rabbits
Science and Nature / Environment and Ecology / Desert / Sonoran Desert
Science and Nature / Zoology
United States / Southwest / Arizona

Printed in the United States of America.